GEOFF BOYCOTT

PLAY CRICKET
THE RIGHT WAY

GREAT NORTHERN

Great Northern Books
PO Box 213, Ilkley, LS29 9WS
www.greatnorthernbooks.co.uk

© Geoffrey Boycott, 1976, 1994, 2010.

Every effort has been made to acknowledge correctly and contact the copyright holders of material in this book. Great Northern Books Ltd apologizes for any unintentional errors or omissions, which should be notified to the publisher.

All rights reserved. No part of this book may be reproduced in any form or by any means without permission in writing from the publisher, except by a reviewer who may quote brief passages in a review.

ISBN: 978 1905 080 694

Design and layout: David Burrill
Photography: Graham Morris (unless otherwise stated)

CIP Data
A catalogue for this book is available from the British Library

This book is based on *Geoff Boycott's Book for Young Cricketers* first published by Stanley Paul in 1976 and the revised edition *Learn Cricket with Geoff Boycott*, published in 1994 by Stanley Paul.

Contents

Preface by John Arlott	5
Introduction	7

Batting
Gripping the Bat	10
The Stance	10
Taking Guard	12
The Back Lift	12
Keep a Straight Bat	12
Playing Forward Defensively	14
Playing Back Defensively	14
The On Drive	16
The Off Drive	16
Attacking Off the Back Foot	16
The Square Cut	18
The Late Cut	18
Cutting Off the Front Foot	18
The Sweep Shot	20
The Pull Shot	20
The Hook	20
The Lofted Straight Drive	22
Moving Out to Drive	22
The Straight Drive	22
Leg Glance Off the Front Foot	24
Leg Glance Off the Back Foot	24
The Full Toss	26
Hitting a Full Toss	26
Yorkers	26
Dealing With Bouncers	28
Facing Fast Bowling	28
Don't Aim for Six	30
Batting in Windy Conditions	30
Batting on a Wet Pitch	30
Loss of Form	32
Play Yourself In	32
Two Shouldered Stance	32
Learn to Relax	34
Don't Waste Your Practice Time	34
Batting One Handed	34
Use a Lightweight Bat	36
Correct Bat Size	36
Choosing Your Own Bat	36
Are Dirty Bats Lucky?	38
New Grips for Old	38
A Batsman's Equipment	38
Reverse sweep	40
The Switch Hit	42

Bowling
Bowling Grips	44
The Basic Bowling Action 1	50
The Basic Bowling Action 2	50
Great Bowlers Use Their Heads	50
Bowling for Beginners	52
Learn to Bowl Straight	52
Don't Waste the New Ball	52
Bowling Against the Wind	54
Bowling at Tall Men	54
Experiment in the Nets	54
The Doosra	56
Reverse swing	58

Fielding
Close-in Fielding	60
Stopping the Ball	60
Attacking Fielding – the Pick-up	62
Attacking Fielding – the Throw-in	62
High Catches	64
Give Yourself Room	64
Catching a Hard One	64
Practice at Playtime	66
Fielding Can Be Fun	66
Cricket for Everybody	66

Captaincy   68

Field Setting   70

Wicket-keeping
Equipment	76
Standing Back	78
Standing Up	78

For the record   80

Geoffrey Boycott hits the runs for his 100th hundred. (Patrick Eagar)

Geoffrey Boycott was a leading light in English cricket for a quarter of a century, making over 48,000 runs and scoring 151 centuries, 22 of them in Test matches.

He was renowned for his mastery of the technical aspects of the game as well as his achievements with Yorkshire and England and the first edition of his book, published in 1976, helped millions throughout the world to become better cricketers. This edition has been brought bang up to date with sections on 'the doosra' and the reverse sweep, two 21st century innovations with a completely new set of illustrations.

The Preface, taken from the original 1976 edition, is written by John Arlott who will long be remembered as a wonderful broadcaster on the BBC and journalist with *The Guardian* who enhanced listeners' and readers' enjoyment of the game over many years. His words on Geoffrey Boycott are still relevant today.

The publishers would like to thank Graham Morris and Patrick Eagar for providing the pictures, Martin Searby for his invaluable help with the manuscript and Steve Oldham and John Blain of Yorkshire for their help in illustrating the various bowlers' grips.

Preface

Geoff Boycott in his great period was the finest batsman in the world; certainly the most dedicated. His batting bears the stamp of careful analysis and construction of method. His right hand is low on the bat, the left effectively high; the left does, positively, lead while the right provides the main propulsive force; and it is all done with quite unusually complete balance of power. His first movement is back and across. He is a careful assessor of the ball, with the great batsman's gift of rarely being in error as to whether to go forward or back. If his batting has one outstanding quality it must be that of quite meticulous placing; he plays through the gaps in a field with greater precision than any other contemporary batsman. The figures of Boycott's batting are convincing enough in themselves; they are even more impressive seen

– as in fairness they should be – against the background of his isolation, of the stress and physical battery to which the target batsman is nowadays subjected.

At five feet ten inches, Boycott is of ideal height for a well-balanced batsman; he is firmly but not heavily built, a coherent mover, strong enough for his purpose and conscientiously fit. His batting is thought out, planned to make the most of his abilities while securing him as completely as possible against the perils to which all batsmen are heirs. He bases his technique on a defence organized as near to flawlessness as can be. Indeed, when he is in form he comes so close to ruling out error that it often seems as if he need never be out. He judges swing well, plays spin with genuine understanding and, despite the battering he has had, scores steadily against pace. At the start of an innings he plays himself in without anxiety, not the least worried if he does not score for half an hour while he takes the pace of the pitch and his measure of bowling. Despite his quick assessment of the bowled ball, he often leaves his stroke quite late, yet without having to hurry it. Then he gradually exerts his range of strokes like a racing motorist opening the throttle and on his great days his batting has an air of inevitability. Geoff Boycott, a superb technician, has – as is well for the team he plays for – an unfailing hunger for batting, runs and success; and his successor is not in sight.

John Arlott

Introduction

Cricket is not an easy game. There are a few fortunate people who seem to take to it and do well without apparent effort but for most of us cricket demands a lot of practice and a willingness to work hard to maintain high standards.

If you want to get to the top or simply play to the best of your ability there is no substitute for practice. Not everyone is cut out to be a county player or reach Test standard but practically everyone who takes up the game can improve his or her performances by perfecting the basic techniques.

It's never too early to start. I went to a coaching school when I was nine and there have been many good players who started before that. If you can get professional coaching, that's the best way; if you can't there is a lot to be learned from watching good players.

Let me emphasize that I advise anyone to play sport rather than watch. It's nice to see youngsters at cricket matches and I think they should be made welcome, perhaps more welcome than they are at some places. But if you have a choice, be a player rather than a spectator.

When you do watch cricket watch the best players – and with your head as well as your eyes.

You will see they all have differences in style and approach but you may also be surprised how many similarities there are, how many basic rules apply to them all. Ask yourself what a player does and why, see if you can spot the difference between one delivery and the next. If the captain makes a fielding change, see if you can spot the reason. In this way you will learn a great deal and enjoy the match all the more.

After all, enjoyment is what the game is all about. Because a professional cricketer earns his living from the game and has an additional responsibility to provide entertainment, he probably takes his pleasures more seriously than the man who plays purely for relaxation. So it should be.

But Sir Donald Bradman once said: 'If the game is not enjoyed, why bother to play it at all?' It took me a while to appreciate the value of that philosophy, but I recommend it to anyone.

Cricket can be something of an inconvenient game because it is time-consuming. Even cricket on the village green usually demands a full afternoon – unless, of course, somebody comes up with a demon bowling performance or one of the umpires has to catch an early bus. But the fact that cricketers are brought together for longish periods helps breed a unique sense of friendship and involvement – not just between team-mates but among rival teams.

This is certainly so in county cricket and local cricket has a special social atmosphere unlike any other game. It's a great way to spend your time.

I am often asked which of my performances have given me the most pleasure over the years and it's not an easy question to answer. Batting well on a difficult pitch for a modest-looking score can be as satisfying as hitting hundreds, but some achievements obviously do stick in the mind.

My first century for Yorkshire was especially sweet because it was scored in a Roses match when we were struggling a bit. The 1965 Gillette Cup final when I scored 146 and helped Brian Close put on 192 against Surrey will always rank high in my memory; then there was that wonderful tour of Australia in 1970-71 when we brought back the Ashes. I have mixed memories about that because I was injured at the end of the tour, but it was a great tour.

My first match for England, being asked to captain Yorkshire, averaging 100 in a first-class season and scoring centuries against every other county and Test country – those are some of the other achievements which have given me pleasure over the years.

One thing is certain – nobody will ever achieve really good, consistent performances unless he masters the basics of the game. And the higher you go up cricket's ladder, the more important that becomes.

When I struggled to find form – and that happens to everyone at some time or another – I concentrated hard on getting the so-called simple things right. I was never afraid to go back to basics because that is where every good performance begins.

This book sets out to help you master the basic ingredients of cricket. I hope you find it interesting and helpful. Work hard at the game and it will repay you in many hours of enjoyment and a real sense of achievement. Believe me, it really is worth the effort.

Wherever I have used the male gender when referring to young cricketers, the comments of course apply to both boys and girls.

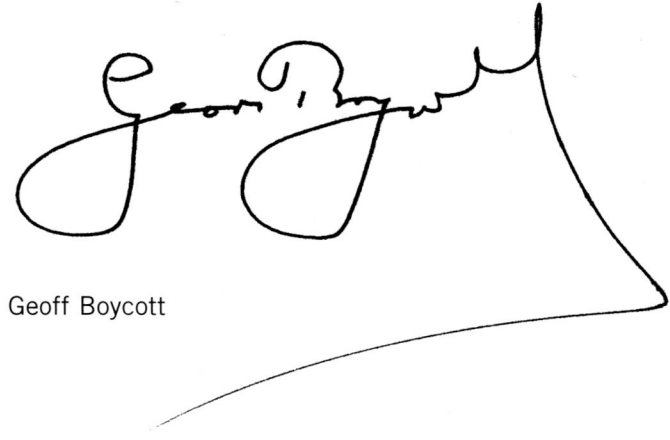

Geoff Boycott

Batting

GRIPPING THE BAT

It is important to have the correct grip to make sure that your hands work together.

Here is a good way to achieve this. Lay the bat face downwards on the ground and pick it up as if you were wielding an axe.

This should give you the natural grip with hands close together on the handle. The Vs formed by the first finger and thumb of each hand will be on the same line, halfway between the outside edge and the splice.

When you face the bowler make sure that the fingers and thumbs of both hands are well round the handle and the back of your left hand faces towards mid-off and extra cover.

THE STANCE

Every batsman must feel comfortable at the wicket and have a relaxed and balanced stance. This is how I faced the bowler.

See how my knees are slightly relaxed with my weight evenly balanced on the balls of both feet for quick and easy movement. My feet are roughly parallel, one on each side of the crease 4" to 6" apart. I found it comfortable to ground my bat just behind my right toes and rest my hands on my left thigh.

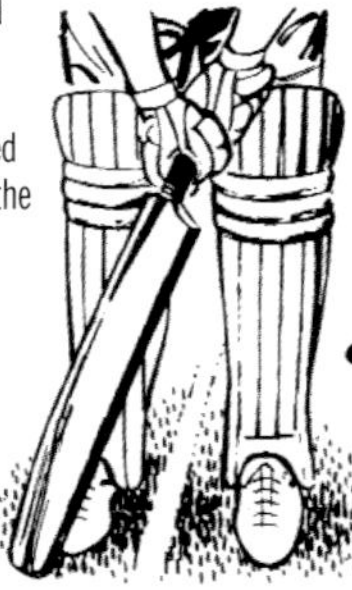

It is most important that the left shoulder should point at the bowler and the head should face down the pitch with eyes looking squarely at the ball.

The beginnning of every good innings. Comfortable, balanced and alert without being tense – a good stance has an air of authority about it as Ravi Bopara shows batting against the West Indies.

TAKING GUARD

When asking for a guard hold your bat upright with its face to the umpire. In this way the umpire can see which stumps it is covering.

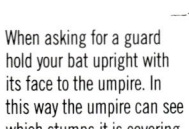

I made sure the umpire gave me guard from behind and over the bowler's wicket because this is the position from where he would make LBW judgements.

Many players ask for a guard 'from where the bowler bowls' – this makes no sense at all.

THE BACK LIFT

A vital part of all batting strokes is the back lift. If you pick the bat up correctly it should go back towards first slip, then loop at the top before coming down straight.

The left arm and wrist do nearly all the work. Notice how my bat is taken back by my left hand and the face of the bat opens towards point.

Lifting the bat back is not natural and it requires hard work to get it right. I used to practise my back lift in front of a mirror and it has helped me to keep a straight bat.

KEEP A STRAIGHT BAT

Most youngsters have difficulty in playing the ball with a straight bat. It is not easy and it requires a lot of hard work to get it right but this simple exercise helped me in my early days.

Drill a hole in a composition ball and thread some wire through it. Fasten the wire to a beam or a tree so that the ball hangs about waist high.

Then concentrate on hitting the ball steadily bringing the bat down straight. If you hit the ball correctly it will return to its original position for you to hit again and again. If it goes off at all angles you need more practice.

12

Everything in line: Kevin Pietersen plays classically forward, bat straight – front knee slightly bent, head over the ball.

PLAYING FORWARD DEFENSIVELY

Every batsman must learn to play forward and stop the good balls from getting him out. Learn to play forward correctly and you are halfway to becoming a good player.

Left shoulder and head lead towards the ball.

Left foot moving to the pitch of the ball.

Let the weight of your body come forward so that the left knee bends slightly and allows the heel of the right foot to ease off the ground. Then as you bring the bat down allow the right hand to relax its grip into the thumb and first two fingers. Look at the angle of the bat as the ball is met just in front of the left foot.

Head over ball

The left hand is always in control so that the ball is met with a straight bat.

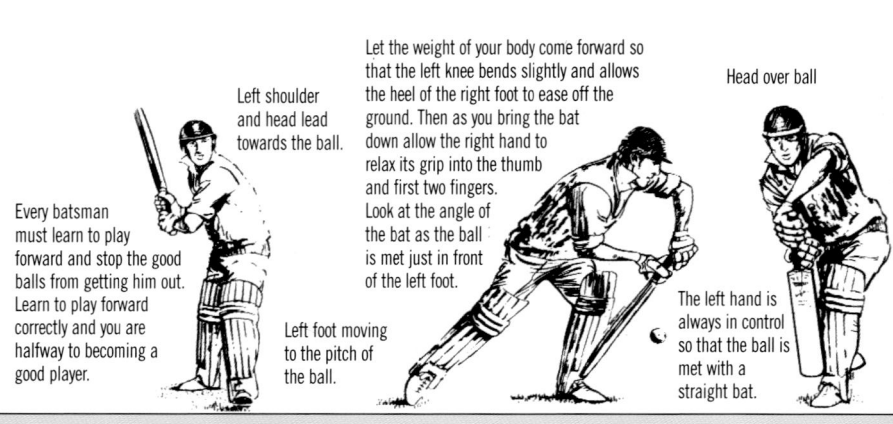

PLAYING BACK DEFENSIVELY

Having played the forward strokes you must learn to play off the back foot if you are to become a consistently successful batsman. All the great players move their right foot well back and across the stumps to bring the head in line with the ball.

Move right foot parallel to the crease to keep the body sideways on to the ball.

By keeping the left elbow high, it is easy to control the bat and allow the right hand to relax into a thumb and finger grip. I allowed my right hand to slide down on to the shoulder of the bat for more control.

Note the angle of the bat.

Head over ball

Finally – let the ball 'come on' to you and meet it with relaxed soft hands so that the ball drops down in front of you.

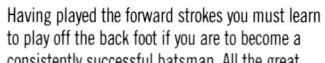

A comfortable big stride, left elbow high, head in line with ball, weight transferring onto the front foot. Alistair Cook shows how it should be done and if you can copy it you're halfway to becoming a good player.

THE ON DRIVE

This is one of the most difficult strokes for young players to master. Make sure that you turn and dip your left shoulder towards mid-on. It will naturally follow that your left foot will open out so that the toes are pointing down the pitch!

Now watch as my left knee bends how the weight of my body is transferred onto my left foot and I hit the ball just inside my left toe.

Here with my left hand in full control I follow through with a straight bat towards mid-on.

THE OFF DRIVE

The most important point about this shot is the movement of the left shoulder which should turn and point towards extra cover. By keeping your head close to the left shoulder, your eyes look down on the line of the ball.

Remember the wider the ball the more you turn your back on the bowler. In this way you make sure you stay sideways on and get your left foot to the pitch of the ball.

Now with the weight firmly on the left foot both arms follow the line of the stroke.

ATTACKING OFF THE BACK FOOT

It should be easy to hit an attacking back foot shot after learning to play back defensively. But young players find this the most difficult shot to play because they will try to hit the ball too hard. This means they throw the head back and scoop the ball up in the air.

Wrong

Be sure to make the most of your height by rising on the toes of your right foot. Then with the left hand controlling the shot, punch at the ball with the right hand just before impact.

Force is not required – the power comes from timing.

Still keeping the head down let the bat follow through in the direction of the ball.

Andrew Strauss shows just how the drive should be played

And driving square off the back foot, a stroke in which control and timing are more important than brute force. Ravi Bopara does it perfectly.

THE SQUARE CUT

When playing the square cut I picked up the bat a little higher and took my right foot well back and across the stumps.

As this is basically a one-footed stroke, keep the weight firmly on the right foot with the toes facing point.

From this position fling the bat down and out to meet the ball. Remember it is essential to come down on the ball from above.

Now as I hit the ball my right knee bent slightly to allow my body weight to come forward into the stroke.

THE LATE CUT

The late cut is a refinement of the square cut and is used to place the ball behind the stumps. There is a pronounced turn of the left shoulder and the right foot lands well back and across the stumps but pointing to third man.

I used to let the ball pass my body so that it was nearly level with the stumps before I met it.

Then with a downward movement of the bat I delicately stroked the ball. Remember you are steering the ball, not hitting it. The pace of the ball will help it on its way.

CUTTING OFF THE FRONT FOOT

To short balls wide of the off stump, young players should play this shot rather than the square cut. It is a natural 'cross' bat stroke and in junior cricket offers the best chance of hitting fours.

Put the left foot well forward with the weight of your body on that foot and throw the bat down and out at the ball with your arms at full stretch.

Always aim to hit the ball at the top of its rise and 'roll' your wrists over to keep the ball down.

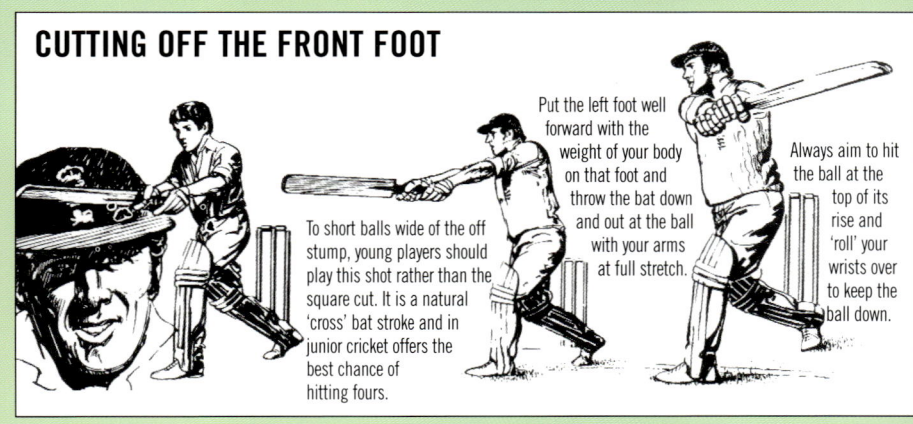

Above left, Mohinder Singh Dhoni is always on the move but is perfectly still when he executes the shot.

Above right, Ravi Bopara forces through the offside off the back foot, a shot he plays exceptionally well.

Right, India's little master, Sachin Tendulkar, has all the shots in the book and here he shows the power of his hooking.

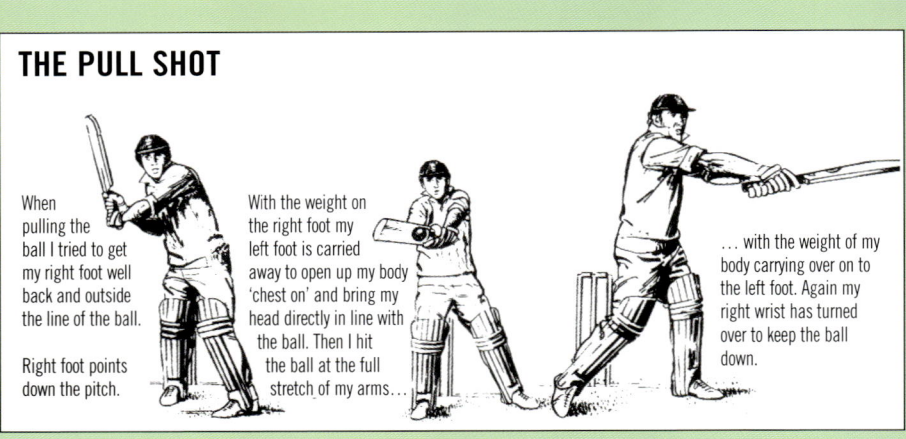

Above left, Paul Collingwood has played some destructive innings. He gets outside the line of the ball and hoicks it over mid wicket with tremendous power.

Above right, Mohinder Singh Dhoni gets chest on to the ball transferring the weight from right to left foot as he pulls in a one-day international against England.

Right, I bet Andrew Strauss enjoyed that. Hooking any bowler for four is a great feeling, particularly when it's Glen McGrath.

THE LOFTED STRAIGHT DRIVE

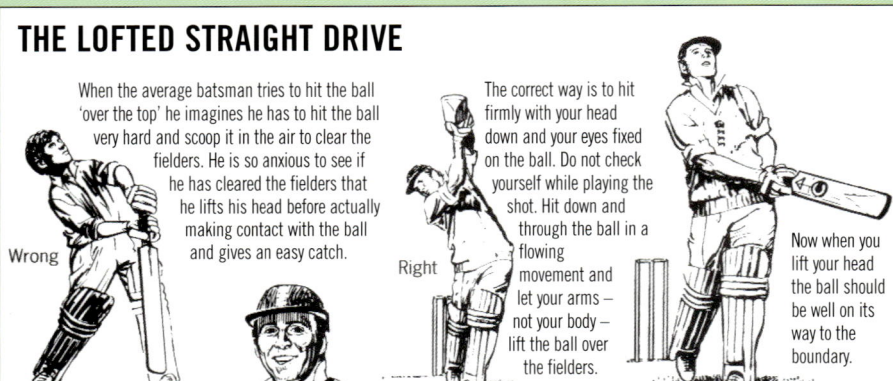

When the average batsman tries to hit the ball 'over the top' he imagines he has to hit the ball very hard and scoop it in the air to clear the fielders. He is so anxious to see if he has cleared the fielders that he lifts his head before actually making contact with the ball and gives an easy catch.

Wrong

The correct way is to hit firmly with your head down and your eyes fixed on the ball. Do not check yourself while playing the shot. Hit down and through the ball in a flowing movement and let your arms — not your body — lift the ball over the fielders.

Right

Now when you lift your head the ball should be well on its way to the boundary.

MOVING OUT TO DRIVE

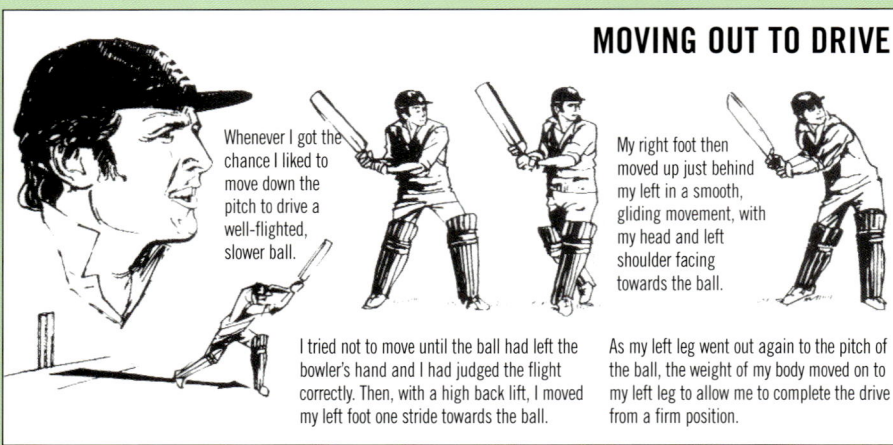

Whenever I got the chance I liked to move down the pitch to drive a well-flighted, slower ball.

I tried not to move until the ball had left the bowler's hand and I had judged the flight correctly. Then, with a high back lift, I moved my left foot one stride towards the ball.

My right foot then moved up just behind my left in a smooth, gliding movement, with my head and left shoulder facing towards the ball.

As my left leg went out again to the pitch of the ball, the weight of my body moved on to my left leg to allow me to complete the drive from a firm position.

THE STRAIGHT DRIVE

If played correctly this is the safest and most rewarding shot in cricket because you are using a straight bat to hit the ball back past the bowler.

With my head and left shoulder pointing at the bowler my left leg went out to the pitch of the ball.

Notice how my left foot points towards mid-off.

With my left arm in full control it is now easy to bring the bat down straight and hit through the ball. As I finish my shot notice how my bat and left arm are still pointing towards the bowler.

A shot we do not see often enough. 'Freddie' Flintoff moves out and straight drives the ball back over the bowler's head.

LEG GLANCE OFF THE FRONT FOOT

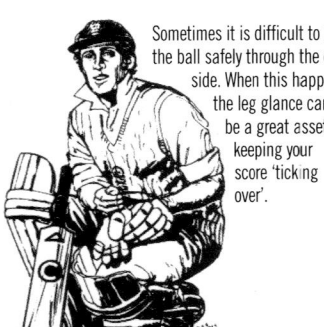

Sometimes it is difficult to hit the ball safely through the on side. When this happens the leg glance can be a great asset in keeping your score 'ticking over'.

To play it correctly you must get the left foot inside the line of the ball so that even if you miss the ball completely it will pass harmlessly down the leg side.

From this safe position turn the face of the bat at the moment of impact and deflect the ball to fine leg.

LEG GLANCE OFF THE BACK FOOT

To play this stroke it is essential that the body opens a little and turns towards the ball. Therefore move the right leg well back and across the stumps with the foot pointing to mid-off.

Bring the left leg close to the right so that if the ball is missed it will hit the outside of the left pad...

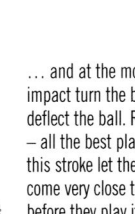

... and at the moment of impact turn the bat face to deflect the ball. Remember – all the best players of this stroke let the ball come very close to them before they play it.

A turn of the wrists at the right moment produces a most delicate shot to the on side from Paul Collingwood.

THE FULL TOSS

Cricket crowds think any full toss is an easy ball to hit but so many batsmen get caught out off a high full toss, because it is almost impossible to get over the ball and hit it down.

When I got a full toss above chest height I played safe and defended. I didn't try to score despite the friendly advice from the crowd to hit it.

If the ball is below chest height then I hit it for runs.

HITTING A FULL TOSS

Most batsmen have strong right hands and feel much happier playing a cross bat shot but so often I see them get out to a full toss. Why? Because they let the ball come too near their body and hit at it with their arms bent.

I made sure I got my head on the line of the ball and the weight of my body on the front foot.

Then keeping my head still I can hit the ball well in front of my left leg with my arms at full stretch.

YORKERS

I've often heard stories of old time greats like W. G. Grace hitting Yorkers for six! I've never seen this phenomenon happen and personally don't believe it is possible.

Remember the ball is pitched near the batting crease so what usually happens when the batsman attempts to drive a Yorker is that he swings over the top of the ball and gets bowled out.

Be content to jab your bat down on the ball to stop yourself from being bowled out. There will be plenty of other balls to hit for runs.

Chris Gayle of the West Indies shows how to deal with the well delivered yorker in the series against England in 2009.

DEALING WITH BOUNCERS

A bouncer is a difficult ball to deal with. However, if you keep your nerve then you shouldn't have too much to worry about.

With a leg side or straight bouncer, duck inside it but turn your head and watch it pass over your left shoulder. You're safe and the bat is well out of the way.

I dealt with bouncers in two ways depending on whether the ball was going down the leg side, straight at me or outside the off stump.

Don't 'freeze' but watch the ball closely and decide whether it is straight – leg-side – or on the off-side.

For an off stump bouncer simply keep upright and sway back – no sense in ducking into it – and watch it whizz by.

FACING FAST BOWLING

Young players often come up against bowling which is much faster than they are used to. You can see them instinctively back away from the ball and play the shot far too late.

When I played against a fast bowler I concentrated on picking my bat up early before the bowler delivered the ball...

... and by keeping a short back lift I gained extra time to play the shot.

28

There is more than one way of dealing with a bouncer. Ian Bell, above, ducks while Paul Collingwood, right, sways away from a nasty one against Pakistan in Lahore.

DON'T AIM FOR SIX

Trying to hit sixes is a common fault of weekend cricketers. By trying to 'whack' the cover off the ball they lift their head and get caught out. Don't consciously attempt six hits. Concentrate on keeping your head down and hitting firmly through the ball.

As a professional I never set out to hit sixes. I aimed to time the ball well and I was sometimes pleasantly surprised when it went sailing over the boundary.

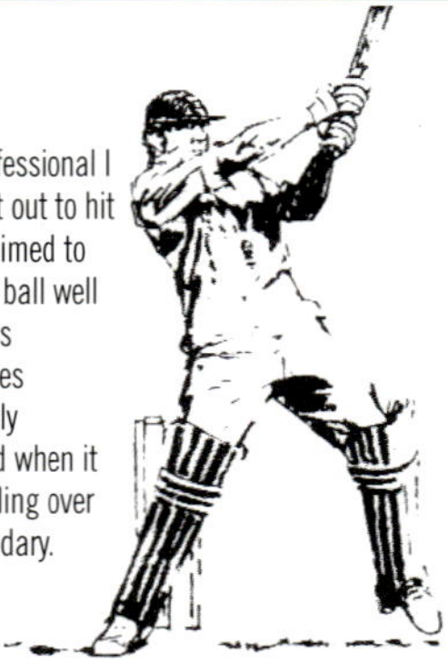

BATTING IN WINDY CONDITIONS

Batting in gusty, windy conditions irritates all batsmen because it upsets their balance and makes it difficult to control the bat. When this happens it is impossible to hit the ball well.

Faced with these conditions I find I kept better control of the bat by using a short back lift.

Then by punching the ball firmly with only a short follow through – it was easier to retain my balance and time the ball correctly.

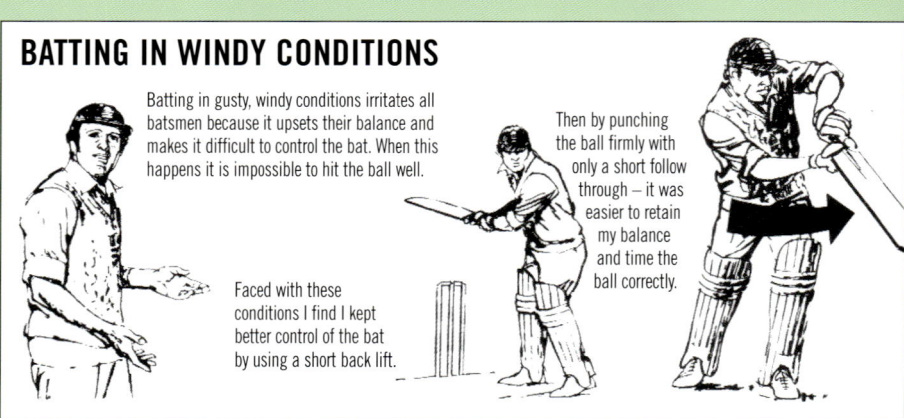

BATTING ON A WET PITCH

Play back whenever possible to give yourself more time to watch the ball.

The last thing you want to do on a wet pitch is drive the ball off the front foot. The soggy turf makes the ball 'stop' and 'lift' so that you 'spoon' a catch to the fielders.

On a wet pitch any ball slightly under-pitched will tend to stand up and wait to be hit! So by staying back I had time to use the square cut, pull and hook shots which are safer and more effective in these wet conditions.

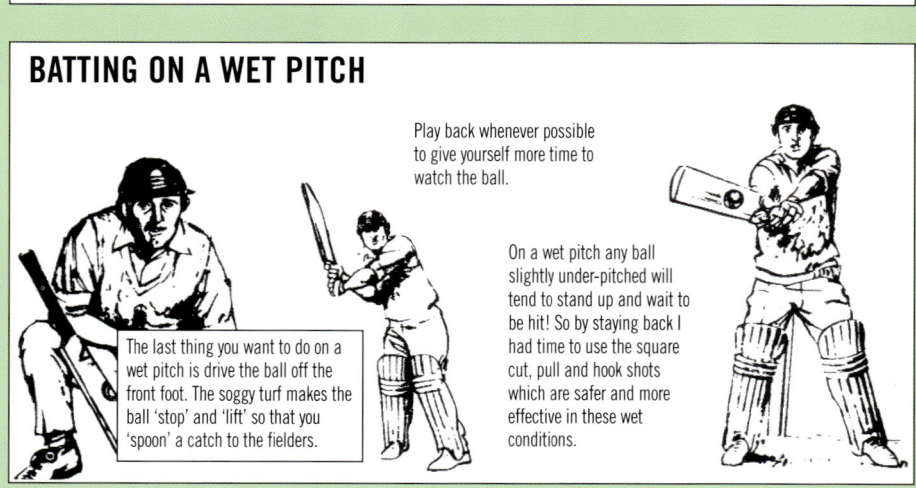

Timing, not brute force, is the secret of a quality stroke as Andrew Strauss demonstrates at Old Trafford.

LOSS OF FORM

All batsmen get out of form at some stage of the season and lose confidence in their ability to score runs. When this happened to me I went back to basics and cut out all the fancy shots.

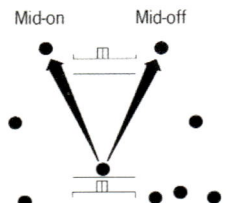

I made myself play in the safety of the 'V' between mid-off and mid-on because all the shots in that area require a straight bat.

By keeping a straight bat I had more chance of middling the ball and less chance of getting out.

PLAY YOURSELF IN

Sometimes batsmen get out because they try to play too many shots at the beginning of their innings. They do not give themselves time to get used to the conditions 'in the middle'.

Always hit the bad ball. But wait until your eyes get used to the light, the bowler's action and the pace of the ball off the pitch before you start playing all your shots.

I kept my score 'ticking over' with singles until I felt confident to play my shots.

TWO SHOULDERED STANCE

If, after a lot of practice, you still have difficulty in dealing with the ball pitched on your legs – don't panic – there is a way round it.

Form a normal stance open your feet and shoulders towards the bowler so that you are 'chest on'.

Shivnarine Chanderpaul uses the two shouldered stance to great effect (the term 'two eyed' stance is incorrect because batsmen use both eyes whichever way they stand at the wicket).

When form and confidence suffer, the only way out is to start at the beginning and concentrate on playing with a straight bat as Michael Vaughan demonstrates.

32

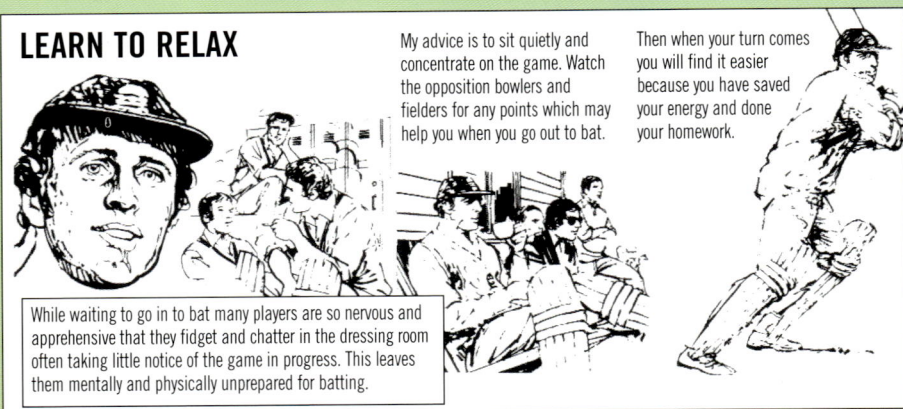

LEARN TO RELAX

My advice is to sit quietly and concentrate on the game. Watch the opposition bowlers and fielders for any points which may help you when you go out to bat.

Then when your turn comes you will find it easier because you have saved your energy and done your homework.

While waiting to go in to bat many players are so nervous and apprehensive that they fidget and chatter in the dressing room often taking little notice of the game in progress. This leaves them mentally and physically unprepared for batting.

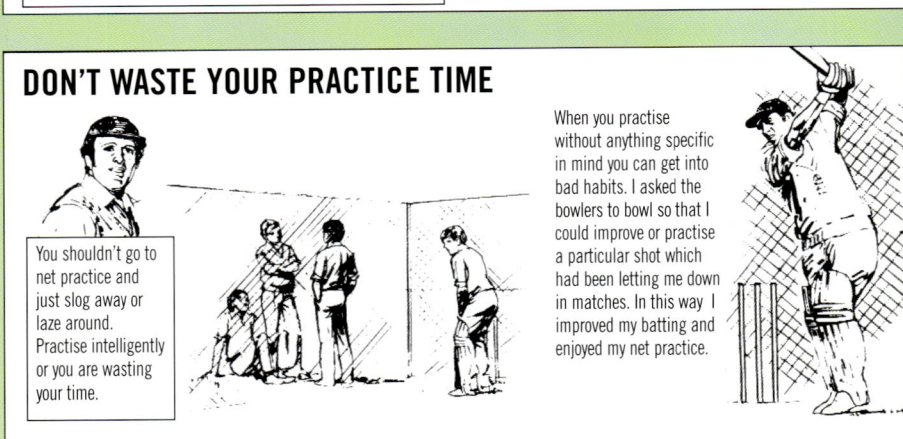

DON'T WASTE YOUR PRACTICE TIME

You shouldn't go to net practice and just slog away or laze around. Practise intelligently or you are wasting your time.

When you practise without anything specific in mind you can get into bad habits. I asked the bowlers to bowl so that I could improve or practise a particular shot which had been letting me down in matches. In this way I improved my batting and enjoyed my net practice.

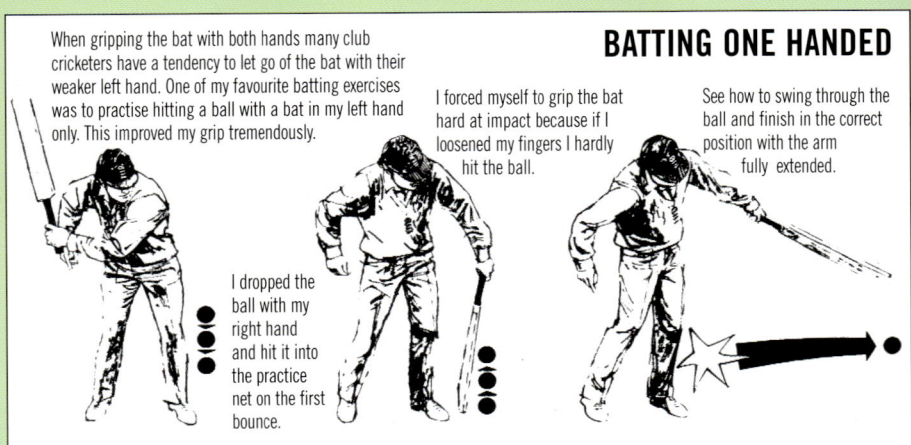

When gripping the bat with both hands many club cricketers have a tendency to let go of the bat with their weaker left hand. One of my favourite batting exercises was to practise hitting a ball with a bat in my left hand only. This improved my grip tremendously.

BATTING ONE HANDED

I forced myself to grip the bat hard at impact because if I loosened my fingers I hardly hit the ball.

See how to swing through the ball and finish in the correct position with the arm fully extended.

I dropped the ball with my right hand and hit it into the practice net on the first bounce.

34

Concentration and a sense of purpose are important in the nets where intelligent practice can help iron out problems. I always enjoyed practice but never did it kitted out like Alistair Cook.

USE A LIGHTWEIGHT BAT

Occasionally people asked me to try out their bats but I nearly always found they were too heavy for me.

A heavy bat is more difficult to control and without control it is impossible to time the ball correctly.

Timing is the secret of hitting the ball well. I used a light bat weighing 2lb 4oz and my advice to the average batsman is to use a lighter bat which is easier to control.

CORRECT BAT SIZE

To bat well you must have the correct size bat. Many young players buy a bat which is too big for them thinking they will 'grow into it' and save themselves some money. This sort of thinking is wrong as it creates bad batting habits which may never be ironed out in later years.

The best way to find the right size bat is to take up your normal stance. The bat should rest behind your right toes – not away from your feet – with the top of the bat handle resting against your left thigh.

If the bat handle rests above the crotch – then the bat is too big for you.

If it is essential to save money, then buy a small bat. Remember, even Sir Leonard Hutton, one of the all time greats, used a Harrow size bat.

CHOOSING YOUR OWN BAT

Many cricketers ask me how to choose a bat. My advice is to take great care in selecting your bat for 'feel' and balance.

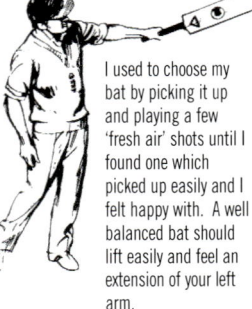

I used to choose my bat by picking it up and playing a few 'fresh air' shots until I found one which picked up easily and I felt happy with. A well balanced bat should lift easily and feel an extension of your left arm.

Remember that no one else can chose your bat for your – buy the one which you 'feel' is right.

Equipment is something for personal taste but to international players like Kevin Pietersen and Andrew Flintoff it is second nature to be properly kitted out in every way. Remember, a bat on the small or light side is less of a disadvantage than one which is too big or too heavy.

ARE DIRTY BATS LUCKY?

I cannot understand any batsman putting his bat away without cleaning it first. After all, a good workman should look after his tools.

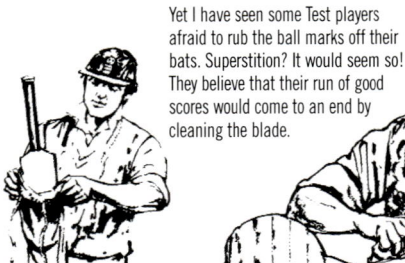

Yet I have seen some Test players afraid to rub the ball marks off their bats. Superstition? It would seem so! They believe that their run of good scores would come to an end by cleaning the blade.

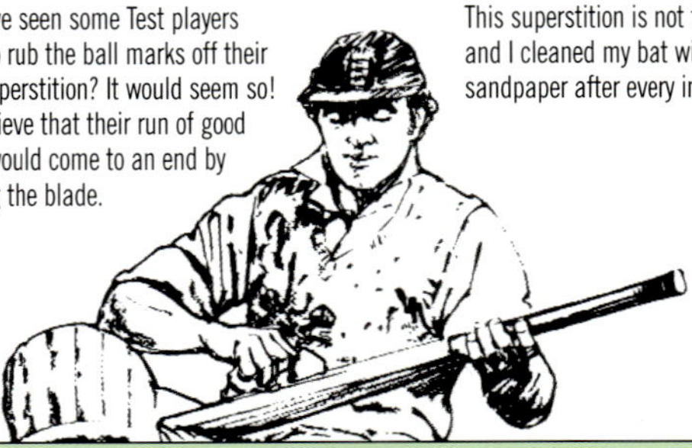

This superstition is not for me and I cleaned my bat with fine sandpaper after every innings.

NEW GRIPS FOR OLD

Sometimes people have asked me to try out a bat but ususally I can hardly hold it because the rubber grip is so slippery.

Very few club cricketers bother about the rubber grips on their bats but I'd hate to think how many runs this costs them each season. Change the rubber grip at the first sign of your hands slipping.

Make sure you use some strong clear glue to make the rubber stick firmly to the bat handle. This will stop the rubber grip revolving round in your hands.

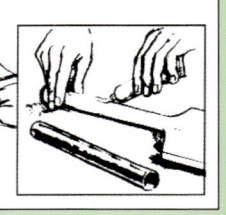

A BATSMAN'S EQUIPMENT

You may think this is a lot of equipment for one batsman but this is what I wore and it helped me to bat with confidence.

- Helmet
- Protector
- Thigh Pad
- Gloves
- Pads

Whether practising in the nets or playing in a match, always wear helmet, pads, gloves, a protector and thigh pads. Remember a cricket ball can be a hard and painful object if you are at the receiving end! This equipment could save you from severe bruising or a crippling injury.

Oh dear! Perhaps Andrew Flintoff, seen here batting for England in a Test match, is one of those with a superstition about cleaning a 'lucky' bat.

The Reverse Sweep

In an orthodox stance you don't change your grip but like all sweep shots play it purely on good length. It came about through one-day cricket to mess up field settings and is usually played to a ball outside the off stump. Turn the bat around but don't try to hit it too hard, just use the pace of the ball.

Mahela Jayawardene of Sri Lanka shows the speed of hand and foot and the judgement needed to play the sweep shot.

Opposite, the reverse sweep should be played strictly on the length of the ball and here South Africa's Ashwell Prince judges it perfectly.

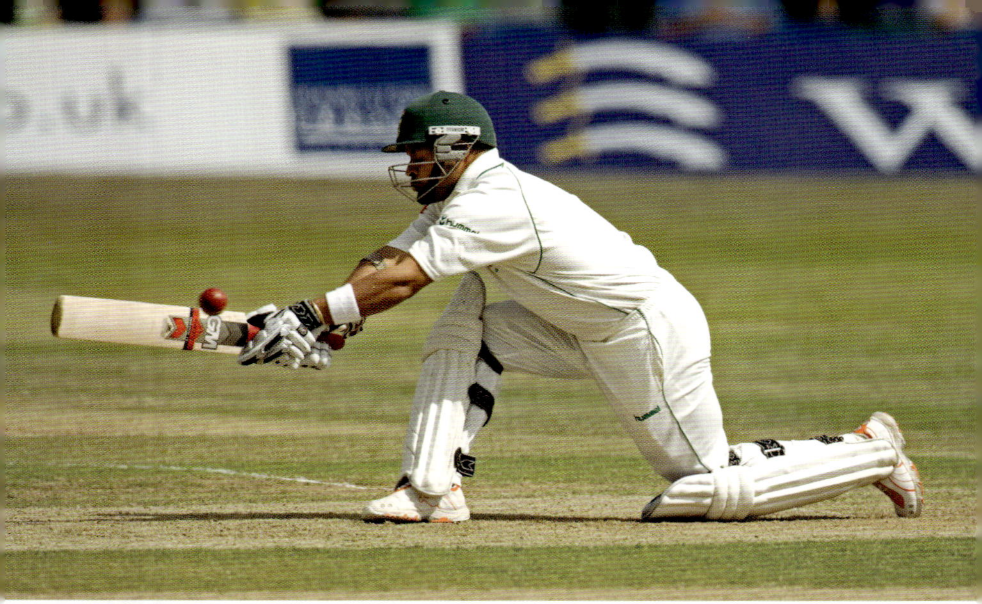

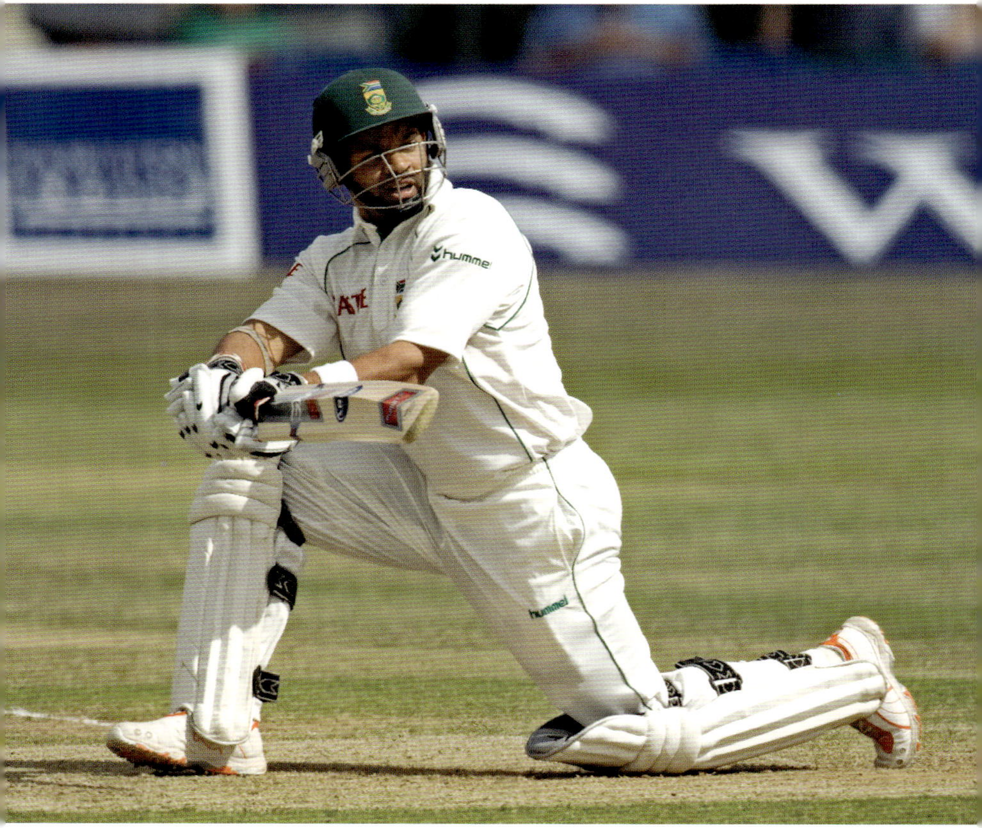
hummel

The Switch Hit

Kevin Pietersen is something totally different. He starts off with a right hander's stance and switches his grip and feet to become a left hander. It takes supreme speed of feet and hands to do it and needs a lot of net practice. It seems impossible to set a field and how can the bowler counter it? The answer is to change your pace and try for a slower ball or a yorker. The batsman usually has to start moving his hands and feet just before the ball is delivered so if you see the batsman start to turn around in his stance, stop and go back to your mark and work out your options.

Kevin Pietersen practises the remarkable 'switch hitting' shot in the nets. It takes supreme speed of hands and feet and is a stroke which perplexes bowlers all round the world. Here we see him in the nets and producing the sensational shot in a Test match.

Bowling

With a new ball and a good bowling action any young person can learn to make the ball swing in the air and move in or out off the seam – provided he or she learns to grip the ball correctly.

A young bowler must decide whether to bowl out-swing or in-swing and set the field accordingly. Both types of swing require different field settings so don't try to bowl both in the same over until you have got control of swing, length and direction – otherwise your bowling may prove expensive and involve risks to your close-in fielders.

Except where indicated, all the grips in this section are for right-hand bowlers. For left-hand bowlers read 'left' for 'right'.

Note – when the new ball starts to lose its gloss, it is vital that all types of bowlers work hard at keeping one side polished and shiny by using sweat and/or saliva.

The grip for right-arm out-swing

Point the seam of the ball towards the slips and place your first and second fingers on either side of the seam. Your third and fourth fingers should curve naturally down the side of the ball while your thumb rests on the seam underneath the ball.

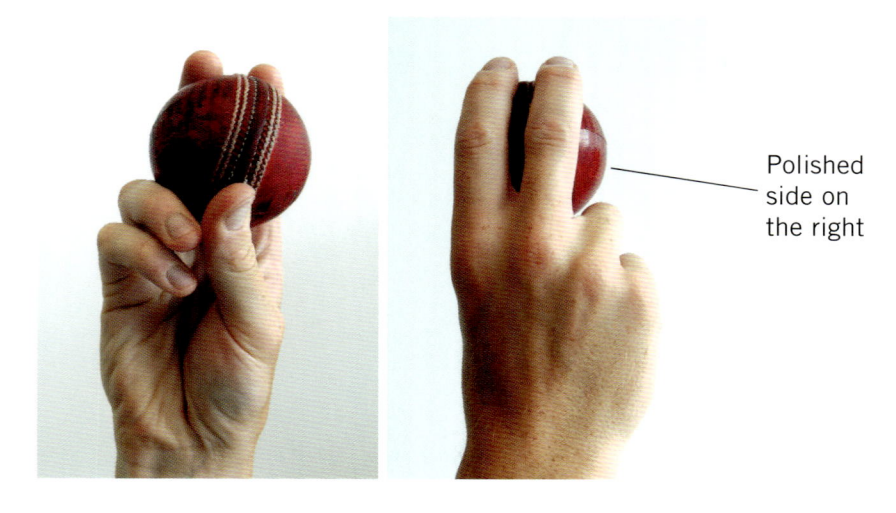

Polished side on the right

The grip for right-arm in-swing

Point the seam of the ball towards fine leg and place your first and second fingers on either side of the seam. Your second finger should lie parallel to the seam while the ball of your thumb rests on the seam underneath the ball. Let your third and fourth fingers curve naturally down the side of the ball.

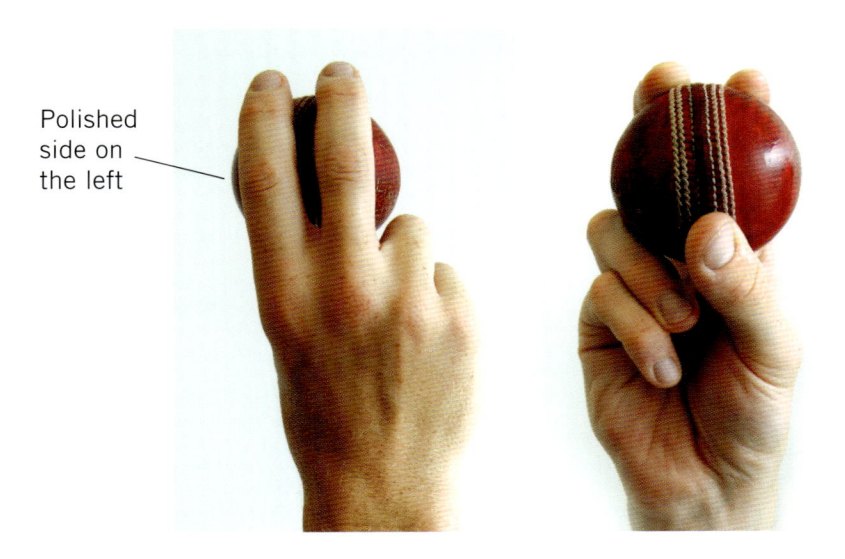

Polished side on the left

Spin bowling

Although all bowlers need to concentrate on bowling good length and direction it is more important for budding spin bowlers to learn to spin the ball first. Experiment and then decide whether you want to be an off-spinner or a leg-spinner because it is difficult to bowl both breaks and difficult but not impossible to set attacking fields for a bowler bowling both types of spin in the same over.

Leg-spin

Space your fist and second fingers comfortably apart across the seam with the top finger joints taking most of the pressure.

Your third and little fingers are naturally below them with the top joint of your third finger lying along the seam and pressing hard up against it.

Keep your wrist cocked inward and as you deliver the ball flick outward and upward with the third finger to impose spin. The action is similar to turning a door knob from right to left.

Off-spin

Grip the ball so that your first finger lies along the seam with the top joint slightly bent and biting into the near edge. This is the main finger which imparts spin.

Your second finger should be spaced comfortably but well away from the first with the other two fingers curled naturally underneath the ball. Your thumb will rest on the other side of the ball near the seam. To spin the ball rotate your hand clockwise much the same as turning the knob to open a door.

Slow left-arm

The grip for the left-arm orthodox slow or slow medium bowler is the same as for the right-arm off-spin bowler, except in reverse, so to speak. Follow the instructions given for the off-spin grip. But note that your hand will rotate in an anti-clockwise direction.

Three different types of spin bowling but they all have accuracy, control and variety. Daniel Vettori, top left, New Zealand's star left arm bowler, above right, England's off spinner Graeme Swann and the incomparable Shane Warne, Australia's magical leg spinner.

49

BASIC BOWLING ACTION 1

A good bowling action is essential, so watch the bowler. His run up is smooth and relaxed as he walks the first pace or two then gradually increases his speed so that only in his last few strides does he reach his full momentum.

In the last but one stride he springs off his left foot and turns his body sideways allowing his right foot to pass in front of the left.

As his right foot lands just behind and parallel to the crease his body is now sideways on to the batsman and he is looking down the pitch from behind his extended left arm.

BASIC BOWLING ACTION 2

In the delivery stride the bowler's body swings forward with the the left arm thrown towards the batsman and the right arm coming upwards, rather like a cartwheel.

To help keep his body in a sideways position his left foot lands pointing to fine leg and directly in line with the right foot. The weight of his body is now firmly on his left leg and his arm is high and ready to deliver the ball.

Once he has released the ball his right arm is carried down and across his left thigh while the left arm swings well back out of the way. He continues to follow through for a few paces to keep his rhythm.

GREAT BOWLERS USE THEIR HEADS

Many people think bowling is just a physical exercise and that bowlers run up to bowl without 'thinking'. All the great bowlers concentrate just as hard as a batsman.

(Thinks) This time I will bowl him a bouncer.

As the bowler walks back to his bowling mark you can see him rubbing a shine on the ball. But all the while he is thinking about what kind of delivery he should bowl next.

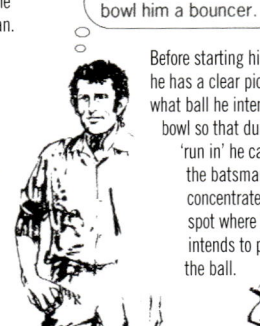

Before starting his run up he has a clear picture of what ball he intends to bowl so that during his 'run in' he can watch the batsman and concentrate on the spot where he intends to pitch the ball.

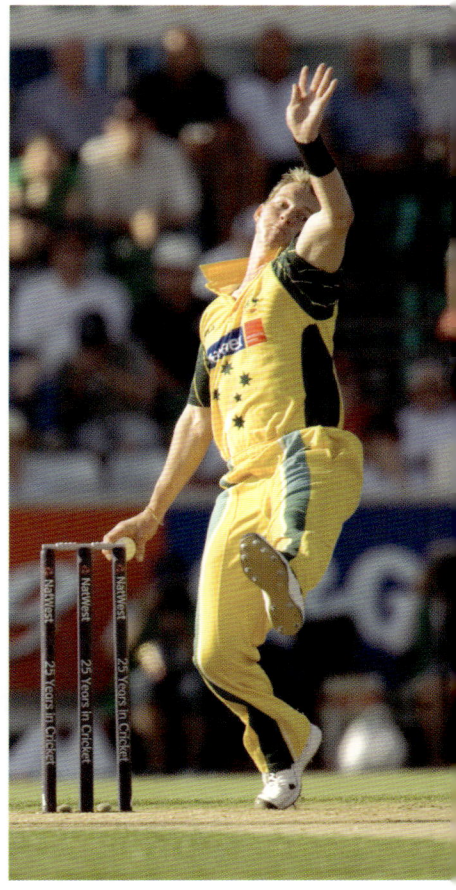

Generating speed and accuracy is not just a matter of racing to the wicket and throwing yourself into a delivery. A good bowling action is smooth and controlled as shown by South Africa's Dale Steyn, above left, and Brett Lee of Austalia.

BOWLING FOR BEGINNERS

Bowling is not a natural action like throwing, but all youngsters can learn to bowl well enough to enjoy themselves if they follow this simple exercise.

Stand with your feet astride and arms sideways. Then rock from one foot to the other keeping your arms outstretched.

Continue rocking with your arms swinging loosely like the sails of a windmill.

Now do this with the ball in your hand and after rocking a few times let the ball go. You are now bowling.

LEARN TO BOWL STRAIGHT

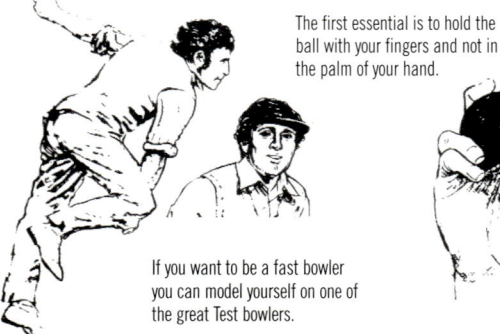

The first essential is to hold the ball with your fingers and not in the palm of your hand.

If you want to be a fast bowler you can model yourself on one of the great Test bowlers.

Secondly, you will have to learn to bowl straight and to do this you must look down the pitch from behind your left arm and shoulder.

Try this simple practice: Chalk some wickets on a wall, mark the crease line and an aiming target in front of the stumps. Then, bowling with a rubber ball, concentrate on hitting the target over and over again.

DON'T WASTE THE NEW BALL

It is a bowling 'crime' to waste the new ball by bowling wide of the stumps so that the batsman does not have to play a shot.

When I opened the innings I was delighted if I didn't have to play the new ball much in the first few overs. It gave me a chance to settle down and get used to the conditions while the shine was going off the ball and the bowler tired, all to no purpose.

At the start of an innings the advantage lies with the new ball bowler — not the batsman. The bowler must retain his advantage by bowling straight enough to make the batsman play.

Accuracy is the fundamental priority of every fast bowler and Australia's wonderful Glen McGrath had it together with subtle changes of pace and length which made him a truly great bowler.

BOWLING AGAINST THE WIND

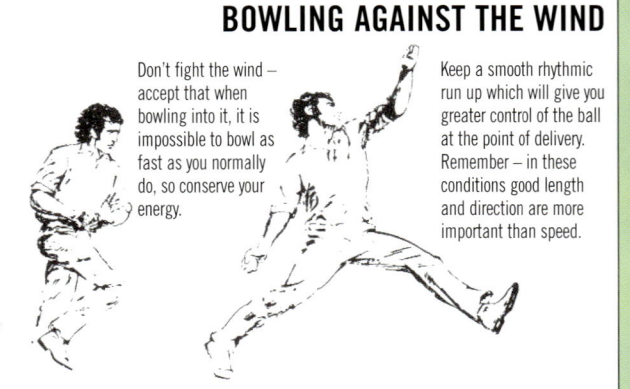

At some stage during the cricket season every fast bowler has to bowl uphill and into the wind. When this happens it's jolly hard work with the wind blowing you backwards as you uselessly strive to maintain your pace.

Don't fight the wind – accept that when bowling into it, it is impossible to bowl as fast as you normally do, so conserve your energy.

Keep a smooth rhythmic run up which will give you greater control of the ball at the point of delivery. Remember – in these conditions good length and direction are more important than speed.

BOWLING AT TALL MEN

Once you can bowl good length balls you must learn to vary your length according to the batsman.

When bowling to a tall batsman an ordinary length ball becomes a half volley and is hit for four. His extra height means he has an enormously long stride and he gets nearer to the pitch of the ball than most batsmen.

In this situation you must make it difficult for the tall batsman to score runs by shortening your length and under pitching considerably.

EXPERIMENT IN THE NETS

At net practice batsmen tend to think bowlers are only there to help them improve their batting. They couldn't be more wrong!

Watch the England bowlers at the nets. They spend the time trying out variations to add to their bowling armoury. Next time you go to practise, experiment. Try something new by attempting to bowl a Yorker, a slower ball, a bouncer, or even try bowling round the wicket.

In the nets many bowlers often bowl at one stump to help them achieve greater accuracy.

For a batsman the advantage of height is being able to turn good length balls into half volleys. Will Jefferson, one of the tallest men in cricket, demonstrates while batting for Essex against Nottinghamshire, the county he joined in 2008.

The Doosra

It literally means 'the second one' and is a new phenomenon which is now part of the game. I don't think it's possible to bowl it without bending the elbow or, to put it bluntly, throwing it. But it is such a fantastic delivery, a ball which looks like an off spinner but which goes the other way, that it is good for the game. You need very supple wrists to try it because the hand has to rotate under the ball to impart the spin. No one does it better than Muttiah Muralitheran, the leading Test wicket taker of all time.

Murali demonstrates his incredibly flexible wrists which allow him to bowl the Doosra as well as the orthodox off spinner.

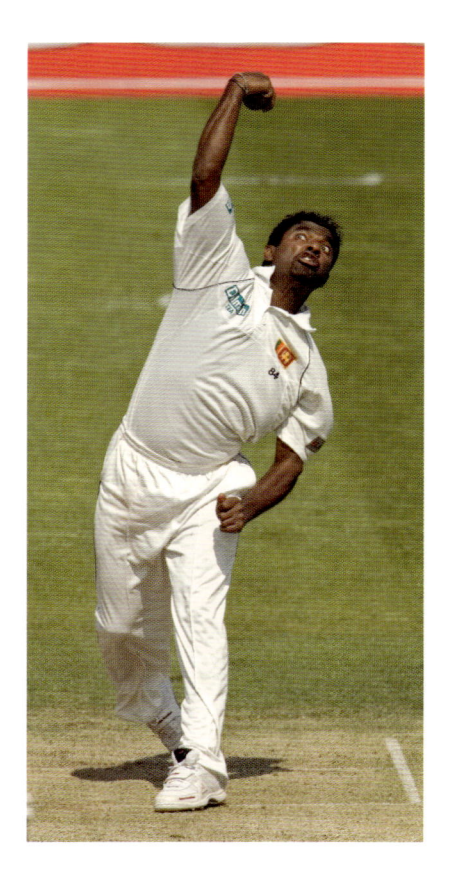

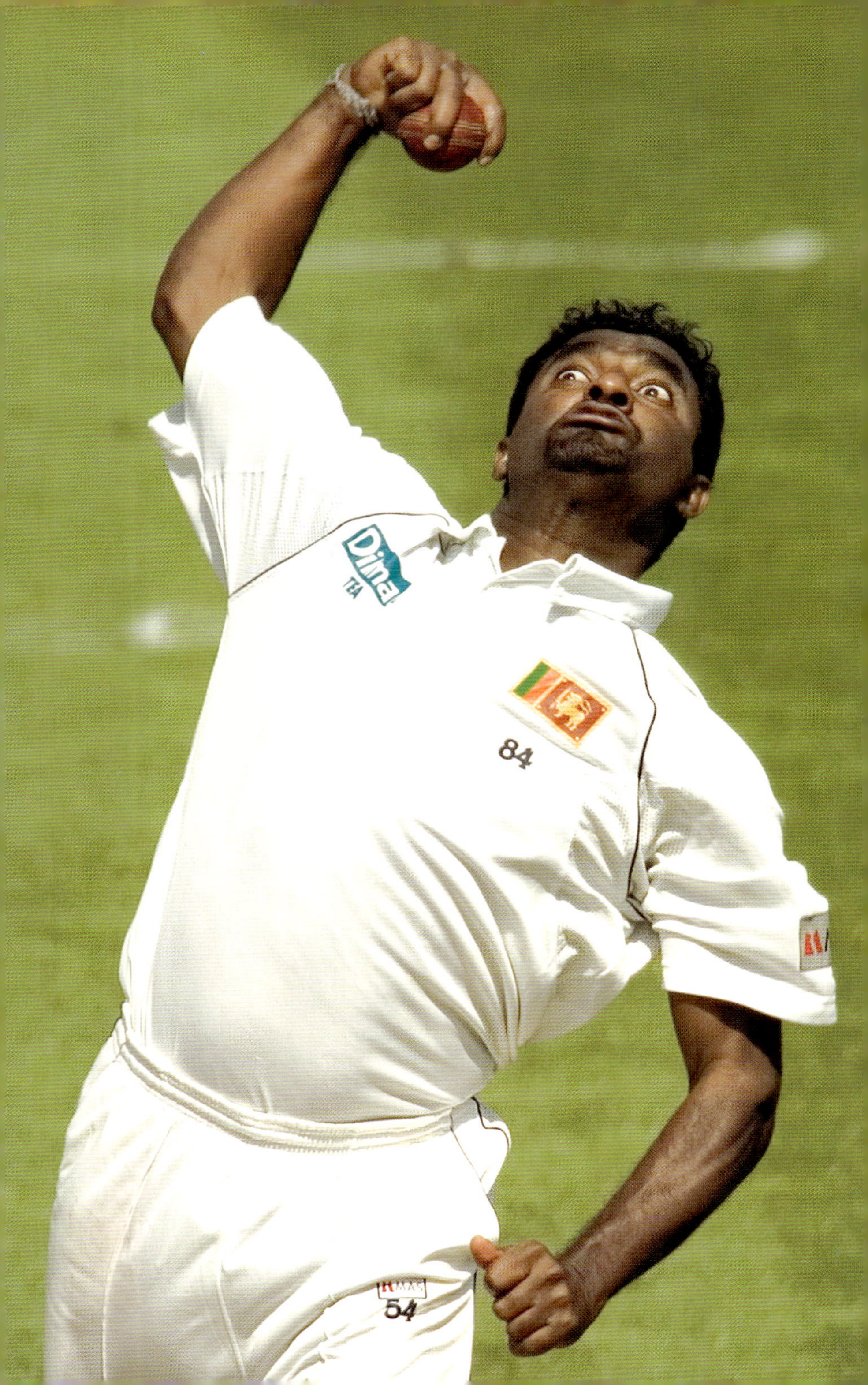
TEA
84
54

Reverse Swing

Normally swing is achieved by using the shiny side of the ball. In-swing, the shiny side is on the left, out-swing the shiny side is on the right. Reverse swing has nothing to do with the shine on the ball and is dictated by the weight on one side, very like the bias in lawn bowls. When the ball gets old and scuffed up one side becomes heavier particularly if sweat is added to it and the heavier side moves through the air more quickly regardless of the shine. To make the ball go in you have to have the rough side on the left; slightly lower the arm so you have a 'slingy' action. If you want to bowl reverse outswing put the rough side on the right but this is much more difficult to achieve.

One of the better exponents of reverse swing, England's James Anderson can move it both ways when the ball is new, in the orthodox fashion, but when it is scuffed up he has another weapon up his sleeve.

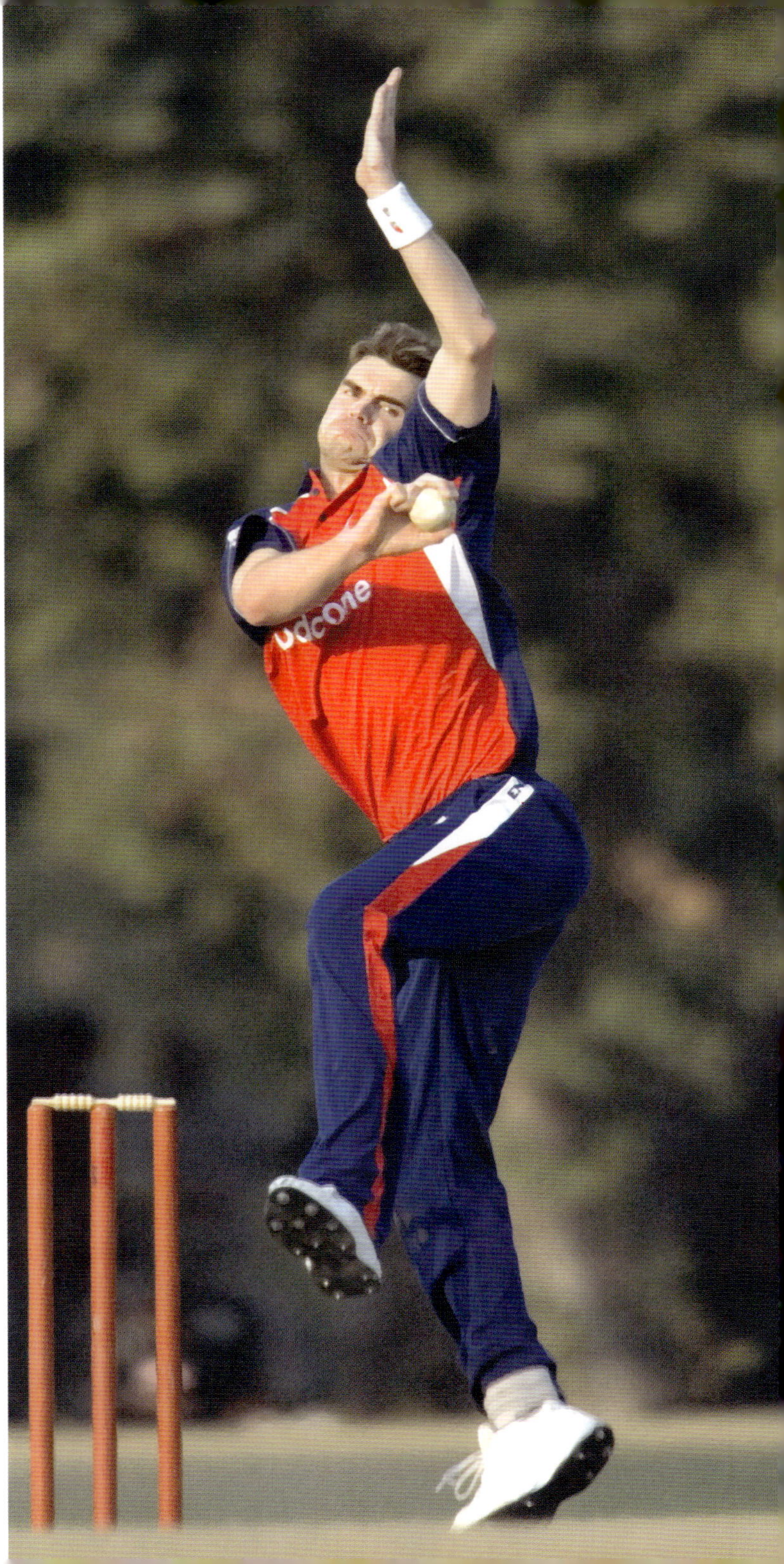

Fielding

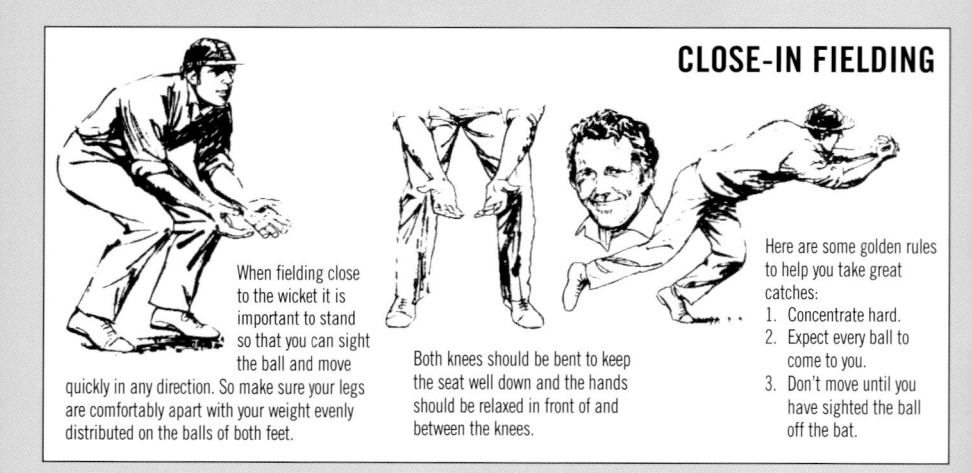

CLOSE-IN FIELDING

When fielding close to the wicket it is important to stand so that you can sight the ball and move quickly in any direction. So make sure your legs are comfortably apart with your weight evenly distributed on the balls of both feet.

Both knees should be bent to keep the seat well down and the hands should be relaxed in front of and between the knees.

Here are some golden rules to help you take great catches:
1. Concentrate hard.
2. Expect every ball to come to you.
3. Don't move until you have sighted the ball off the bat.

STOPPING THE BALL

When fielding, the first job is to stop the ball with your hands, but if that fails, with some other part of your body. To make sure of doing this you must get your body behind the line of the ball in either of the following ways.

Meet the ball chest on with your heels together and toes apart. Bend your knees to allow the body to get well down and receive the ball in front of your feet with the fingers pointing down.

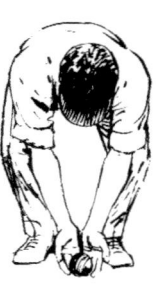

Many professional cricketers prefer to meet the ball sideways on. By dropping onto the left knee and opening up the right foot the body presents the maximum barrier to the oncoming ball. The hands take the ball in front of the left thigh. Fielding has developed due to the one-day game and the sliding stop has become a regular feature.

They can come at all heights and angles when you field in the slips. Paul Collingwood shows how concentration and alertness pay off while Andrew Strauss clings on to an absolute crackerjack

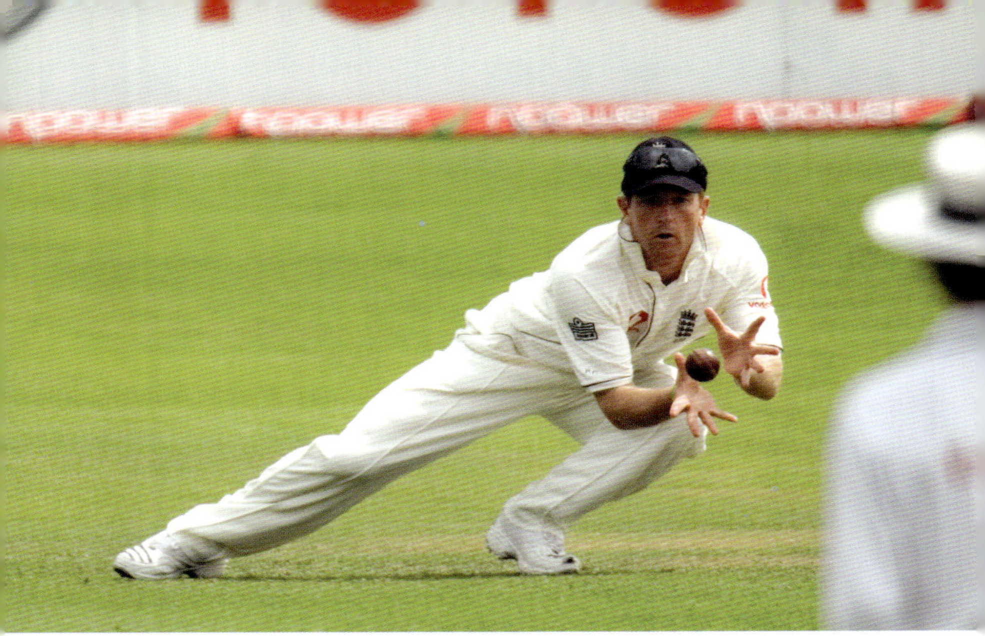

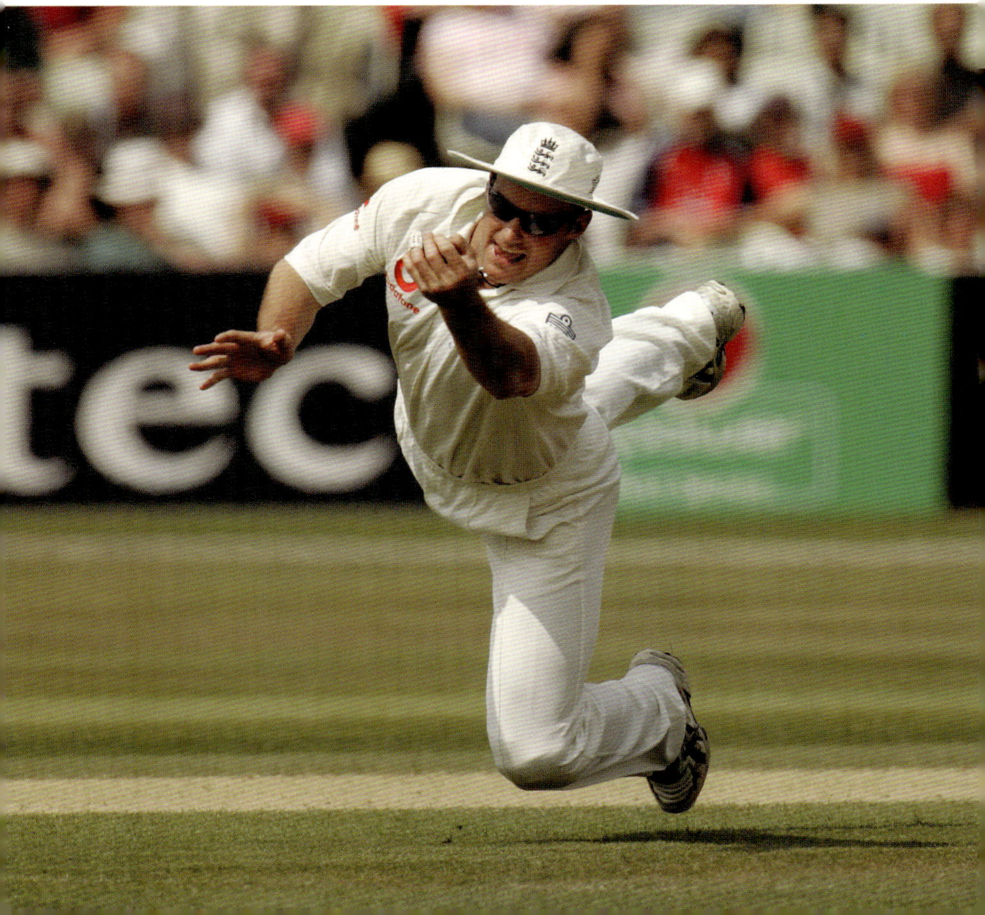
tec

ATTACKING FIELDING – THE PICK-UP

When you can stop the ball, learn how to save runs by attacking fielding. Always watch the batsman – not the bowler – and as the ball is bowled walk in slowly so that you can accelerate in any direction to meet the ball.

Now watch me. As I reach the ball, my body turns sideways so that my right foot in its final stride lands at right angles to the line of the ball.

With the weight firmly on my right foot my hands move down to receive the ball just in front of my right toe. I never take my eyes off the ball until it is safely in my hands.

ATTACKING FIELDING – THE THROW-IN

Once I receive the ball in the attacking fielding position my body is naturally placed for aiming a fast 'throw-in'.

So from here I take my right arm – with wrist cocked – straight back until it is in line with my right shoulder and at the same time point my left arm straight at the target. By using the left arm as an aiming device I can achieve greater accuracy and lessen the chance of making a 'wild throw'.

As I throw the ball the weight of my body automatically transfers onto my left foot and with the ball speeding on its way my right arm is pointing down the line of flight.

All fielding requires practice no matter at what level you play. Kevin Pietersen, above left, gets his eye in, James Dalrymple, above right, of Glamorgan shows how to watch the ball and get your hands out early for a catch in the deep and Stuart Broad, right, watches the ball into his hands.

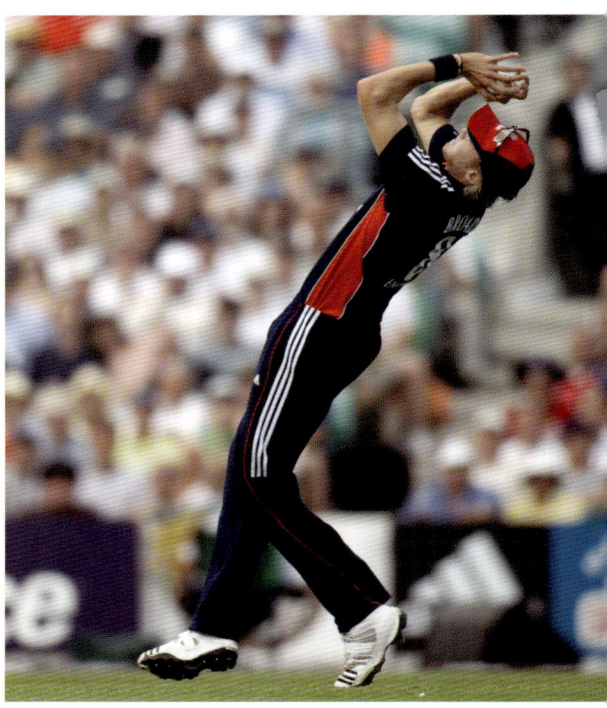

Young cricketers when faced with this situation are frightened to catch the ball for fear of being hurt, but if you follow these simple instructions you have nothing to worry about.

HIGH CATCHES

Spread your hands and fingers in a wide relaxed web and catch the ball at the base of the fingers.

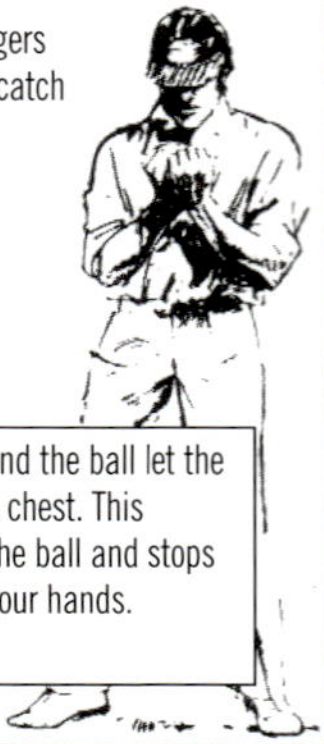

1. Don't move until you have sighted the ball then get under it quickly.
2. Once there, keep your head still and watch the ball.
3. Then raise your hands early enough to catch the ball at about eye level.

As the fingers close around the ball let the hands 'give' towards the chest. This cushions the impact of the ball and stops it from bouncing out of your hands.

GIVE YOURSELF ROOM

I'm not surprised this young man dropped the ball. It came at him straight and fast like a bullet and he got his hands to the ball all right — but out it bounced! By standing still and trying to catch it in front of his body his hands had no room to 'give' with the ball.

When faced with this situation I moved my body slightly to one side of the oncoming ball…

… so that as I took the catch my hands had room to 'ride with the ball'. This cushions the impact and stops it from bouncing out of my hands.

CATCHING A HARD ONE

I think the most difficult catch to take is when the ball is hit hard and flat and coming straight for your head as it is impossible to catch the ball in the normal way.

When taking this catch make a 'web' of your hands with the fingers pointing upwards then move your head slightly to one side — still keeping your eyes on the ball.

Now as your fingers close around the ball you have room to let your hands 'ride with it' towards your shoulder. If you meet the ball with rigid hands it will bounce out.

Balance and reflexes personified as 'Freddie' Flintoff dives to take a one-handed catch in the NatWest Final at Lord's and Dwayne Bravo of the West Indies is perfectly poised to hold a skier, something which always looks easier than it is.

PRACTICE AT PLAYTIME

You can always improve your 'ball sense' if you are keen enough. Here is a simple example of how to improve your catching and throwing.

If you are at a loose end on your own, chalk a target on a wall, stand a few yards away and throw a rubber ball at the target — catching it as it bounces back.

If you have a friend willing to play with you stand a few yards apart facing the wall. Using the same target throw and catch the ball in turn.

To improve your slip fielding and quicken your reactions try this game. Two people face a wall at a distance of some 4 to 6 yards. A third person stands behind them and throws a rubber ball at the wall. The two people facing the wall have to sight and catch the ball on the rebound.

FIELDING CAN BE FUN

Fielding is the easiest and most natural of all cricket activities. But you can't call yourself a cricketer until you are a good fielder.

Have a bit of fielding practice in front of the pavilion before the start of every match. Even Test cricketers have a few minutes warm up before they take to the field. It gives them a chance to get the feel of the ball.

When your team takes the field don't treat it as a chore — go out meaning to enjoy yourself. Good fielding will inspire your team and help the bowlers by saving runs and creating a run out.

CRICKET FOR EVERYBODY

You often see a game of cricket between youngsters with one or two talented players doing all the batting and bowling. Those who do nothing but field soon get bored and drift away from the game into some other activity. Here is a game of cricket which gives everyone an equal chance at batting, bowling, wicket-keeping and fielding. Spread out in these positions.

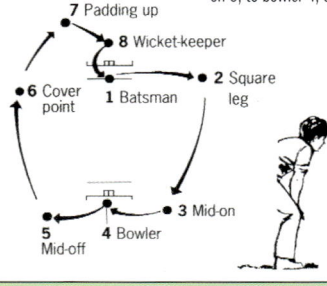

7 Padding up
8 Wicket-keeper
6 Cover point
1 Batsman
2 Square leg
3 Mid-on
4 Bowler
5 Mid-off

Each batsman receives two overs then everyone changes round clockwise: wicket-keeper 8, to batsman 1, to square leg 2, to mid-on 3, to bowler 4, etc.

By continuing in this way everyone is kept interested and enjoys the game.

Slip catching practice has become an ever more important part of every team's preparations. They used to use a slip catching cradle but here England's Ian Bell warms up with a slip catching machine which fires a ball at different heights and angles.

Captaincy

Captaincy has been described as a gift, an acquired skill, an art and a science, but whichever way you look at it, captaincy plays an important and sometimes vital role in cricket.

When a side wins a captain is given special credit; if a side loses it is not uncommon for the captain to be blamed. Human nature being what it is nobody wants to admit to playing badly, so everybody tends to look for a scapegoat – and the captain can come under fire from batsmen, bowlers and fielders alike. Even spectators usually reckon they could have done a better job.

Because of this there may be a tendency to try to please everybody – but resist it. Too much well-meaning advice from your players and outsiders can only complicate matters for you. If you are going to take responsibility for decisions do yourself justice by making them yourself. In other words, have the courage of your convictions.

That does not mean you cannot benefit from the experience and knowledge of others. When you feel it necessary, confer with your vice-captain and accept a little help from your players. You are always learning at this game and a captain has to be willing to learn faster and more often than any of his players. But a captain has to be positive and decisive, even when there are half a dozen awkward factors which have to be weighed in his decision.

If you don't always feel absolutely certain that your decision is right – and that is bound to happen if you are honest with yourself – at least look and act in a positive fashion. Keep a cool head, don't get ruffled or show you are worried and above all don't change your mind with every delivery or the team will soon become uncertain and lose confidence in you.

On the other hand a captain has to be flexible, to keep an open mind and try to suit his tactics to a game that can change by the minute. It is not a crime to change your mind, provided that you think changes through and don't make them in an atmosphere of panic.

Always give encouragement when you feel it is due, although sooner or later you will have to be critical of the team and individual

On the attack. Every England man is around the bat in a vain effort to force victory in the West Indies in 2009.

performances. That is inevitable and an important part of any captain's responsibilities.

Try to be constructive in your criticism, remembering that individuals are likely to react in different ways. Don't be afraid to be forceful when a point has to be made but guard against the kind of criticism which makes a player feel resentful.

Study the personalities of your own team as closely as you study the opponents' strengths and weaknesses. Your technical ability as a captain is entirely a matter of your own performance and experience but you can become a really good leader if you discover how to make a team work together.

It's a difficult job for which there is no easy formula, no straightforward method which any textbook can teach. It's very much up to you.

Field setting

Out-swing, right arm

(a) Good Pitch

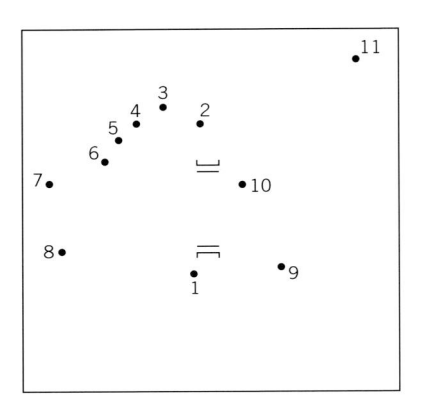

(b) Slow or wet pitch, with the occasional ball 'stopping'

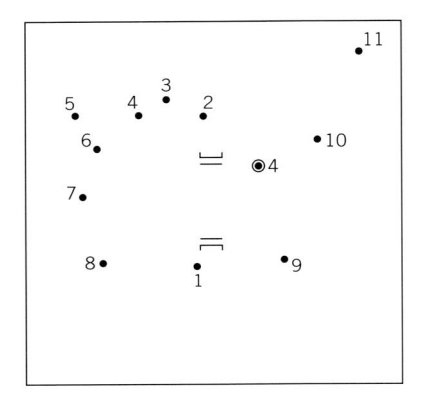

1. Bowler
2. Wicket-keeper
3. First slip
4. Second slip
5. Third slip
6. Gully
7. Square cover point
8. Wide mid-off – more or less extra cover
9. Mid-on
10. Bat-pad
11. Fine leg

1. Bowler
2. Wicket-keeper
3. First slip
4. Second slip
5. Short third man
6. Gully
7. Square cover would move to a more orthodox cover position in front of the wicket
8. Mid-off would move straight
9. Mid-on
10. Leg gully to catch the occasional ball which 'stops' or 'pops'
11. Fine leg

In-swing, right arm

(a) Good Pitch

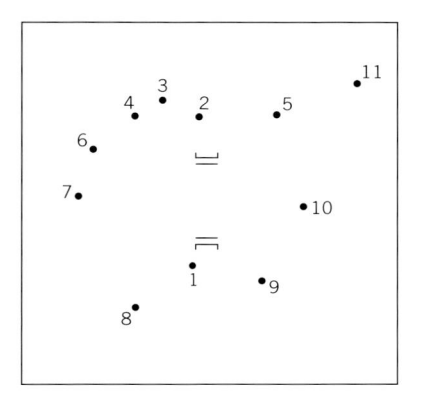

(b) Slow or wet pitch, with the occasional ball 'stopping'

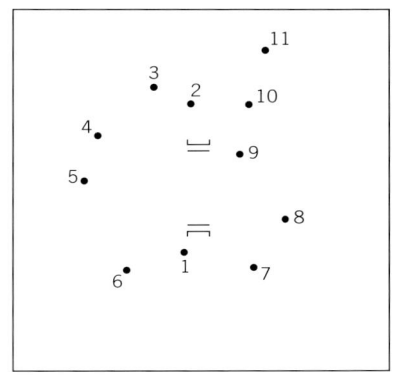

1. Bowler
2. Wicket-keeper
3. First slip
4. Second slip
5. Leg gully
6. Gully
7. Cover point in front of square
8. Straight mid-off
9. Mid-on
10. Mid wicket
11. Fine leg wide of leg slip

1. Bowler
2. Wicket-keeper
3. First slip
4. Gully
5. Cover point in front of square
6. Straight mid-off
7. Mid-on
8. Mid-wicket
9. Slip would go to short square leg ⎤
10. Leg slip would go square or wider ⎦ Both to catch the ball which lifts off a length
11. Fine leg would move finer or 'inside' the leg gully

Left-arm swing bowling over the wicket

(a) Good pitch – new ball, attacking field

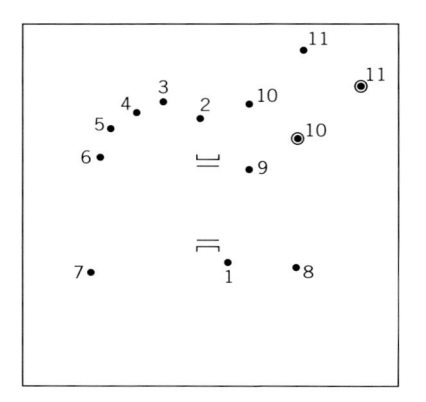

(b) Slow or wet pitch – occasional ball 'stopping'

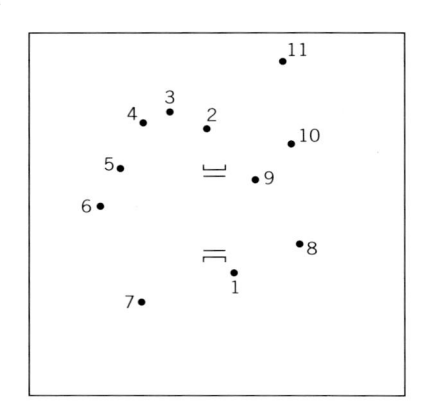

1. Bowler
2. Wicket-keeper
3. First slip
4. Second slip
5. Wide third slip
6. Gully
7. Extra cover or wide mid-off saving the single
8. Wide mid-on or straightish mid-wicket saving the single
9. Bat-pad
10. Leg slip – vary position
11. Fine leg outside leg slip or inside wide leg gully

1. Bowler
2. Wicket-keeper
3. First slip
4. Second slip
5. Gully
6. Cover
7. Extra cover moves straighter to mid-off
8. Wide mid-on or straightish mid-wicket saving the single
9. Square leg to short square leg
10. Leg gully moves squarer or wider
11. Fine leg moves inside the leg gully

Off-spin, right arm

(a) Good Pitch

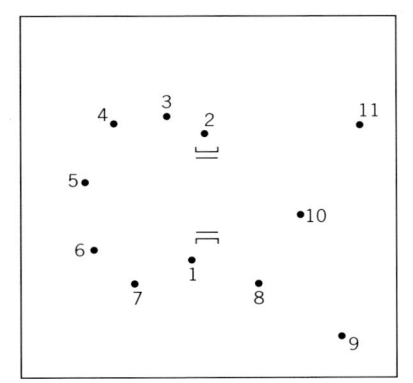

Off-spin

(b) Spinning pitch – attacking field

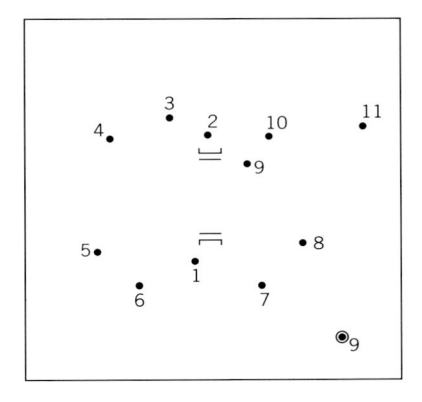

1. Bowler
2. Wicket-keeper
3. Slip
4. Short third man saving a single
5. Cover point
6. Extra cover
7. Mid-off
8. Mid-on
9. Deep mid-wicket – straight
10. Mid-wicket
11. Backward square leg saving a single, three quarters of the way to the boundary. That way has a chance of catching a top edge sweep

1. Bowler
2. Wicket-keeper
3. Slip
4. Short third man saving a single
5. Extra cover
6. Mid-off
7. Mid-on
8. Straight mid-wicket
9. Forward short leg should crowd the new batsman but once the batsman starts hitting out I suggest he be removed to deep mid-wicket
10. Leg gully
11. Backward square leg only three quarters of the way to the boundary to catch top edge sweep.

Leg break, right arm
(a) Good Pitch

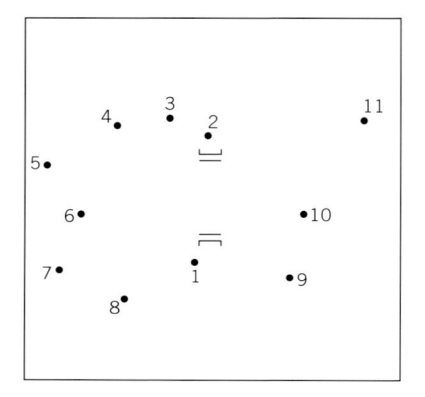

Leg break
(b) Slow pitch, 'turning a bit'

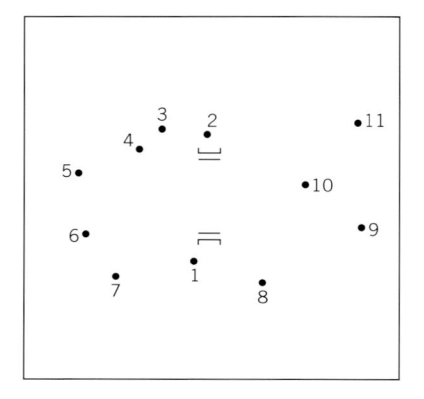

1. Bowler
2. Wicket-keeper
3. Slip
4. Short third man saving a single
5. Squarish cover point. The offside field should be staggered
6. Extra cover saving a single
7. Deepish extra cover
8. Mid-off not too near
9. Mid-on
10. Mid-wicket
11. Deep square leg behind square

1. Bowler
2. Wicket-keeper
3. Slip-wider ⎤ Both slightly
4. Short third ⎦— nearer than on
   man to gully   a good pitch
5. Squarish cover point
6. Extra cover saving a single
7. Mid-off now saving the single
8. Mid-on
9. Deep mid-wicket
10. Mid-wicket
11. Deep square leg just behind square

Left arm slow bowling around the wicket

(a) Good Pitch

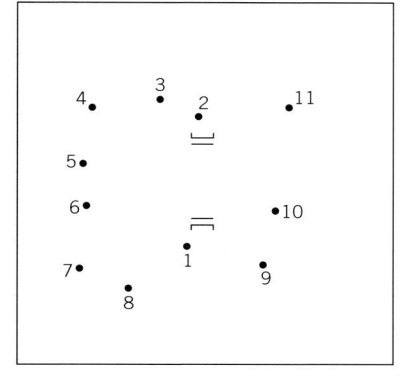

(b) 'Turning' pitch – attacking field

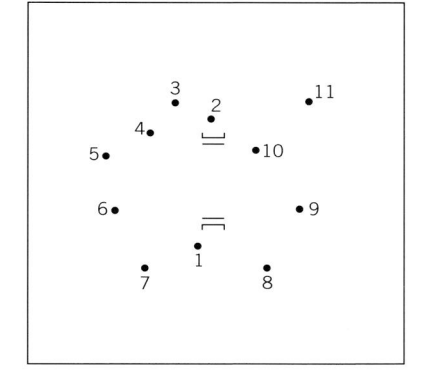

1. Bowler
2. Wicket-keeper
3. Slip
4. Short third man saving a single
5. Cover
6. Extra Cover
7. Deepish extra cover
8. Mid-off
9. Mid-on
10. Straightish mid-wicket
11. Short fine leg saving a single

1. Bowler
2. Wicket-keeper
3. Slip
4. Gully
5. Square cover
6. Extra cover
7. Mid-off
8. Mid-on needs to be a little deeper
9. Straightish mid-wicket
10. Short square leg
11. Short fine leg saving a single but if batsman sweeps needs to be put back three quarters of the way to the boundary

Wicket-keeping

Alan Knott of Kent and England was one of the all-time greats, and in my view the best wicket-keeper ever. He said: 'Wicket-keeping is hard work but wonderfully rewarding because you are never out of the game.'

There are two chief essentials for keeping wicket – an ability to sight the ball early and then to catch it, whether it comes from a ball bowled, a hit or a throw-in.

On taking the ball you must 'give' a little with the hands, reducing resistance and the risk of the ball jumping out of the gloves. This 'give' also helps prevent bruising. Relax your hands and try not to keep the fingers rigid; they should form a padded cup into which the ball will sink.

Dismiss from your mind any thought that the ball is going to hit the the stumps, the batsman's body or even go for runs, and build up your powers of concentration to the point where you believe and expect every ball is coming through to you.

Equipment

The most important part of any wicket-keeper's equipment is obviously his gloves, and the choice is a matter of personal preference. Some keepers like a supple pair with hardly any cushioning so that they feel the ball as much as possible; others prefer a heavy, well-padded pair for protection. Use the ones with which you feel happy and comfortable.

Whichever you choose I advise all youngsters to use a pair of cotton or chamois inners. Dampen them to make them pliable but don't oversoak them. They make for more comfort and may prevent your hands becoming bruised, which is absolutely essential. If your hands do become bruised you may reach a point where you do not want the ball to come to you and that is a hopeless situation.

Finally, always wear an abdominal protector: it's the commonsense way to avoid a serious injury.

Agility is essential in a wicketkeeper and, above, Matt Prior leaps athletically to take the ball. Right, South Africa's Mark Boucher shows perfect balance and positioning in a one-day international against England.

Standing back

Most keepers like to take the ball about waist height and that determines how far back they stand. The aim should be to take a good-length ball just after it begins to drop its trajectory towards you after pitching.

Position yourself wide of the off stump so you can see the ball all the way from the bowler's hand; don't tuck yourself too far behind the stumps or you will not see balls pitching on the leg stump because of the batsman's body.

A wicket-keeper standing back must always be ready to go for any catch he reckons he can take, boldly and without hesitation. And that applies regardless of the position of the slips.

Standing up

Most young wicket-keepers feel a bit apprehensive about standing up to the wicket in case the ball is deflected sharply and hits them. This is perfectly understandable but with practice and concentration and wearing a helmet with a visor there is no real need to worry.

Squat down so that your view is not restricted by the batsman's body and keep your head as close to the line of the off stump as possible – the closer the better. Then you will have a good view and be in a position to whip off the bails without stretching or the need for a short pace, which costs valuable time if a stumping chance comes along. Obviously, you should not be so close to the stumps that your movement is restricted by them.

As each delivery rises from the pitch your hands should follow the course of the ball. Never move back from the wicket. If the ball is wide of the stumps move your outside foot sideways to bring head and body across and behind the line.

As soon as you have taken the ball you should be ready to take off the bails. To become a quick stumper you must develop the habit of bringing your hands back towards the wicket after every delivery – even if the batsman has played it. Go through the motions until they become second nature, then you will not have to hurry when a real stumping

Adam Gilchrist of Australia owed much to the time spent 'keeping to Shane Warne but he was very sharp and never afraid to stand up.

Mark Boucher also had quick hands and here he whips the bails off in a flash to send back 'Freddie' Flintoff.

opportunity occurs.

A wicket-keeper's general attitude and alertness can rub off on the rest of the team. A workmanlike, confident keeper can contribute a great deal to a team's overall performance.

When taking returns from fielders get into position behind the stumps as quickly as possible. Face the fielder and no matter how wild the throw try to take it tidily and before it bounces – never stop it with your pads. If a catch is skied near the wicket, the keeper obviously has a big advantage over other fielders because of his gloves. He should shout 'mine' or preferably 'keeper' so that nobody is left in doubt that he intends to make the catch.

Every wicket-keeper makes mistakes – he is so involved in the play that it would be a miracle if he didn't. But don't dwell on missed chances and let them affect your performance during the rest of the innings. Study the cause later by all means, but try to forget misses once they have happened and concentrate on the next delivery.

Remember you are looking for reliability and consistency. Sometimes you will produce a really magic moment of which you will be justifiably proud, but there is nothing worse than the keeper who is spectacular and brilliant one day and hopeless the next.

For the record

Of all the players who have scored over 26,000 runs in first-class cricket, Geoff Boycott has the second highest average (after Sir Donald Bradman) – 48,426 runs at 56.83. He scored 151 first-class centuries, which is the fifth highest, and played in 108 Test matches for England, scoring 8,114 runs at 47.72.